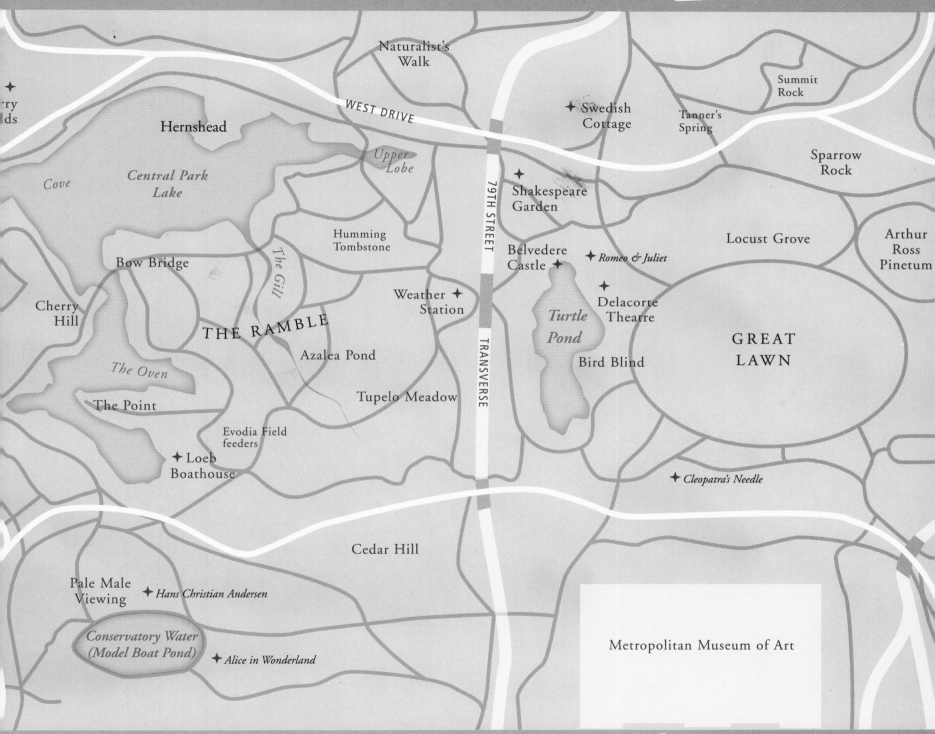

Naturalist's
Walk

WEST DRIVE

Summit
Rock

Hernshead

✦ Swedish
Cottage

Tanner's
Spring

Sparrow
Rock

*Upper
Lobe*

Cove

*Central Park
Lake*

79TH STREET

✦ Shakespeare
Garden

Humming
Tombstone

Belvedere
Castle ✦

✦ *Romeo & Juliet*

Locust Grove

Arthur
Ross
Pinetum

Bow Bridge

The Gill

Weather
Station ✦

*Turtle
Pond*

✦ Delacorte
Theatre

Cherry
Hill

THE RAMBLE

TRANSVERSE

GREAT
LAWN

The Oven

Azalea Pond

Bird Blind

The Point

Tupelo Meadow

Evodia Field
feeders

✦ Loeb
Boathouse

✦ *Cleopatra's Needle*

Cedar Hill

Pale Male
Viewing

✦ *Hans Christian Andersen*

*Conservatory Water
(Model Boat Pond)*

✦ *Alice in Wonderland*

Metropolitan Museum of Art

5TH AVENUE

A true conservationist is a man who knows that the world is not given by his fathers but borrowed from his children.

—John James Audubon

Birds
of
Central
Park

TEXT AND PHOTOGRAPHY BY CAL VORNBERGER

FOREWORD BY MARIE WINN

HARRY N. ABRAMS, INC., PUBLISHERS

For my brother, Bill, who is always there when I need him.

TABLE OF CONTENTS

FOREWORD

THERE'S AN INFORMAL little community of bird watchers, butterfly and dragon-fly fanciers, wildflower, mushroom, tree and you-name-it identifiers who spend a lot of time in Central Park. They're known as the Regulars. You don't have to join this group to belong. You just have to show up regularly, in the heat of summer and the freeze of winter, at sunrise, sunset, or any time in between, day after day, year after year.

I've been a Regular since Pale Male, the cover bird of this book, first arrived in the park. That was fifteen years ago. But most of us couldn't tell you when Cal Vornberger first joined us. He simply became part of the environment, like a tree in the woodlands that you've never looked at before. Suddenly you notice it, and you can't be sure it hasn't always been there.

That's what happened with Cal. At some point during the last three or four years we realized that this quiet, friendly, unobtrusive man was always there. If he hadn't already set up his tripod to take pictures, he'd have his huge telescope slung over his left shoulder. On his back he'd be carrying a super-sized black backpack bearing extra lenses, batteries, meters, tools, a level, a tele-extender, a plastic garbage bag that doubles as an emergency raincoat, cleaning materials, and a little container of Tylenol for "those days." I once tried to lift this backpack. I couldn't move it, even with both hands.

Though he is not a real bird watcher—he is the first to admit it—from the start we understood that this man's interest in birds was as deep as ours, though different. He doesn't have the passion for identification that animates most of the Regulars. But for reasons as mysterious as for most of our passions, he is driven to photograph wild birds in this urban park. And in order to accomplish this difficult task, he has spent thousands of hours observing them in their natural habitats. In the course of time he has come to know almost as much about birds as the best bird watchers do.

Cal's book uniquely captures an aspect of Central Park that I and my kindred spirits there treasure: the mystery and excitement of the changing seasons. The Woodcock in the snow on page 11 represents one of the highpoints of a Central Park bird watcher's winter. When this long-billed woodland-loving shorebird shows up in late February, weeks before the songbird migration begins, it is an eagerly welcomed harbinger of spring.

Everybody knows that spring in Central Park is a madhouse of tanagers, orioles, thrushes, vireos, cuckoos, and over thirty species of warbler. But only those who've watched winter turn into spring will fully appreciate the tenderness of the newly-emerged, shiny pin-oak leaves that surround the Baltimore Oriole on page 82.

Fall is epitomized by birds eating berries. But after decades of watching flickers feeding on berries in early October, I've never once caught sight of a flicker flicking his tongue like a snake, as in the photo on page 184.

Summer is family time for birds in Central Park, and

Robins are the park's most prolific nesters. Sometimes they'll make their home in the most unexpected places, as in the statue of Romeo and Juliet pictured on page 98. But only an insider will find a Wood Thrush feeding a fledgling in the Ramble, a rare and gratifying bird happening in the park (see page 102). And only someone who knows exactly where to go could have captured that valiant Red-winged Blackbird on page 125, shooing a Great Egret ten times its size from its nest at Turtle Pond. That's one of my favorite pictures in the book.

The various birds you'll find portrayed on the pages of this remarkable collection all appear so artistically arranged on their branches or fence posts or hollow logs, their colors so vibrant, their actions so dramatic—foraging for food, taking off in flight, braking for a landing, singing, staring you straight in the eye—that you might imagine each of them flying in for a prearranged sitting at the photographer's studio. He artfully positions each subject on its proper perch with its appropriate accessory: the Night Heron with his fish, the Herring Gull with his bagel, the Yellow Warbler on her spray of cherry blossoms. He adjusts his focus to achieve absolute sharpness. He sets up his lights to bring out each bird's finest colors. Then he gives them their instructions: "Okay, now burst into song," or "Hey, cock that head a little more to the left."

I remember the last time I saw a collection of birds portrayed with such clarity. It was an illustrated article about songbirds in the magazine section of my Sunday newspaper. As I stared at the perfect portraits of some of the most elusive of our warblers, I saw that indeed they were too perfect. They were dead. Though the article never said so, these were photographs of stuffed birds! It was a scandal that caused much amusement in the bird watching community.

There is no question that the birds in this book are alive; indeed, they sometimes seem to be bursting out of their assigned pages. A mystery remains, however. Over the years, most of us have managed to find these birds for ourselves as we wander through the park. But we usually see them for a split second only. They're often partially hidden. This photographer shows them right out in the open!

How does he do it? If he doesn't pose them in his studio, if he doesn't stuff and mount them, does he play a magic flute that charms them out of their hiding places, like Papageno in the Mozart opera?

Here's what I think must be the secret behind Cal Vornberger's photographs: He's a tree in human disguise. Take a good look at him. He's a sturdy, strong tree of a man. He wears grayish baggy pants the color of a hackberry trunk, and a maple-brown corduroy jacket. Even his telescope sports a brown-and-green-spotted sleeve that resembles the bark of a sycamore tree. He has a short beard that might, from a distance, be taken for grey lichen or moss. When you come upon Cal in some corner of the park you don't immediately notice him. He's rooted to the spot, as it were. Like a tree.

Now we're closing in on the secret of this photographer's mastery. Of course it takes a combination of elements to produce a beautiful photograph of a bird: You need technical know-how, artistic talent, and, perhaps, the right equipment. But first and foremost among this knowledgeable, gifted man's battery of skills may be the ability to stand stock still for many minutes, even for hours. The bird he is stalking finally figures out that the guy's a tree, and comes out into the open. It proceeds to sing, catch an inchworm, scratch its belly, or do something else picturesque. For Cal Vornberger, patience, almost beyond human understanding, is the magic flute.

INTRODUCTION

THE QUESTION I'm most frequently asked is, "Why photograph birds in Central Park?" The Central Park part is fairly easy, the photography part a little more complicated.

Central Park is a bird magnet. It's located on the Atlantic flyway so hundreds of thousands of birds moving up and down the East Coast during spring and fall migration pass directly over it. Because many of these birds migrate at night, the first thing they see as dawn breaks is a vast green oasis in the middle of a sea of concrete. They are hungry and exhausted, and on high the park looks like a perfect place to rest and replenish before beginning their journey again.

Central Park is, in fact, an oasis for migrating birds: Seeds, berries, fruits, and insects provide a smorgasbord for just about every bird imaginable. Even the park's large rodent and pigeon population is much prized by hungry predators such as hawks and owls. No wonder author and ornithologist Roger F. Pasquier, writing in *Travel + Leisure*, cited Central Park as one of America's top bird watching locations. In fact, more than 200 species of wild birds are regularly seen in Central Park and, although the park's first official bird census in 1886 listed only 121, in subsequent years more than 282 separate species have been observed in the park. Recently a Boreal Owl—a bird never before observed in Central Park—was spotted in a tree next to Tavern on the Green. This shy native of Canadian boreal forests is rarely seen on its own breeding ground, much less in Central Park.

The park's popularity is so widespread that birders from all over the world flock there during spring and fall migration. One crisp spring morning I counted more than 150 birders in the Ramble alone. Among these were bused-in birders from Pennsylvania, several couples from Great Britain, and a dozen youngsters from a local school.

Visitors to Central Park who are interested in finding birds should check the Bird Book located in the Loeb Boathouse next to Central Park Lake. It contains reports of bird sightings that are updated every day by local birders. The American Museum of Natural History and several individuals offer bird watching walks in spring and fall. Check my Web site (http://www.birdsofcentralpark.com) for more information about these walks and other Central Park birding news, or visit Mike Freeman's excellent site, New York City Bird Report (http://www.nycbirdreport.com) for up-to-date information about sightings in Central Park and other New York City locations.

Why I like to photograph birds is probably a cause of being exposed to nature and photography at an early age, as well as being an avid reader of Patrick O'Brian's nautical fiction. O'Brian is, in my opinion, one of the great writers of the twentieth century, whose work was almost entirely unknown until the final years of his life. Some critics have compared him favorably with Jane Austen, but most people know O'Brian as the author of the book behind the Russell Crowe film *Master and Commander*. That movie is, in fact, a concatenation of two O'Brian novels: *Master and*

Commander and *The Far Side of the World*. Readers of the twenty works in the Aubrey/Mautarin series quickly realize that both O'Brian and his hero, Stephen Mautarin, are ardent natural philosophers with a keen interest in all forms of wildlife. Each book contains many detailed descriptions of the birds observed by Dr. Mautarin as he travels the world on a series of British Royal Naval vessels commanded by his particular friend Jack Aubrey. The only time I was lucky enough to have an extended conversation with O'Brian, it revolved almost entirely around the birds of the eastern United States as compared to those in southern France, where he lived.

I gained an early love of nature growing up in a northern suburb of Detroit in a new development of tract houses that was near a large lake and adjacent to several acres of heavily forested undeveloped land. In spring and summer we caught tadpoles and garter snakes. There were robins everywhere. In fall we raked leaves into great big piles and jumped from trees into them. In June there was a small patch of tiny, honey-sweet wild strawberries that my friends and I would gather. In July and August we stuffed ourselves with blackberries, and in September with apples from an old, abandoned orchard nearby.

My father was a semi-professional photographer who took photos during World War II (we found boxes of them under his bed after he died) and ended up taking photos of crime scenes and automobile accidents for the police force in the town where I grew up. He had a darkroom in our basement where he would process and print the police department photos and his own work. When I was old enough he let me take photos with his vintage twin-lens reflex. He taught me how to develop and print

black-and-white film, and when, at sixteen, I was selected to go to Chile as a foreign exchange student, he bought me a 35mm camera and a couple of nice lenses. When I returned home the local newspaper printed two of my photos.

I continued to shoot in black-and-white and process and print it. In college I majored in theatrical design and took lots of photos of my productions. I eventually ended up in New York City working as a theatrical and television designer. During that time I continued to take photos of my work, my travels, and my friends, but I never considered doing anything serious with photography.

For the next twelve years I established and ran an interactive agency in Tribeca. I sold the company in 2000 and found myself with a lot of time on my hands, but, unfortunately, not the hoped-for financial independence. So I decided to do something I'd often dreamed of: become a professional photographer. I already had a small but well-regarded body of work, loved to travel, spoke several languages, and felt comfortable living and working in other cultures so I decided to specialize in travel photography.

When I got off the plane in New York in the summer of 2001, I had the beginnings of a travel portfolio in the hundred-plus rolls of film I had shot in Spain and France. Combined with my recent shots of New York City and some well-placed contacts among former clients, I thought I might just make a go of it.

As I was organizing and scanning my European photos, I got a call from a friend. Had I heard the news? An airplane had crashed into the World Trade Center. Soon after, I was talking to that same friend, and she remarked that she would not be doing any traveling for a while. I suddenly realized that neither would anyone else. My career as a travel photographer was over before it began. It didn't seem like such a big deal, though, compared to the larger tragedy.

In late October 2001 I decided to take my camera and go for a walk in Central Park. On this foray I took my 35mm camera and a couple of wide-angle lenses and walked across 104th Street to the park. I took a few shots of the fall foliage as I walked south, but my heart really wasn't in it. I wandered down to Turtle Pond and walked out onto the observation deck. There, off to the right, was a large white bird wading in the water and catching fish with its long yellow beak. I was amazed! Although my lens was not long enough to give me a decent image of the bird, I snapped away. The bird flew off to the far end of Turtle Pond and I snapped. The bird flew back and I snapped. The bird flew off again and I snapped. Back and forth, back and forth, this went on for at least an hour before the egret finally flew off for good. I took six rolls of thirty-six exposures that day, knowing full well the bird wasn't close enough for me to get a decent shot.

I asked someone on the deck about the bird. It was a Great Egret and fairly common there this time of year. I was hooked and was determined to get a good photo of this bird. The next day I came back with a slightly longer lens but, given the type of photography I had been doing, I didn't own a lens that was up to the task. However, the lens was the least of my problems—the egret wasn't at Turtle Pond! I walked over to Central Park Lake and he wasn't there either. There were a lot of ducks, geese, and a couple of swans, though, so I spent the afternoon shooting them. They were pretty tame and I could get close enough for frame-filling shots, but I couldn't forget that egret.

That evening I bought a copy of Petersen's *Birds of Eastern and Central North America,* and the only book I could find on photographing birds, Arthur Morris's *The Art of Bird Photography*. I kept searching for the egret that fall but never found him again. I went to the park almost daily throughout the fall and winter, and by spring I had bought larger lenses and a digital camera body. I spent the spring photographing egrets, herons, and other birds in the park.

I showed my shots to Arthur Morris during a wildlife photography class I took with him that spring. He offered lots of encouragement and was impressed I decided to "go digital." Because of my background in digital technology I was right at home in the digital darkroom. All the photographs in this book were color corrected, scaled, cropped, and sharpened on my Mac and PC at home.

In late spring, summer, and early fall I prefer working in the early morning and late afternoon because the sun is lower on the horizon and my photographs will have less contrast and greater dynamic range. I also like the color and quality of light at these times. When I do shoot with the sun higher on the horizon I use my flash and flash extender (see Equipment, pages 202–203) to fill the underside of the subject and lessen contrast.

On a typical summer's day I get up around 4:00 a.m., and I am out before sunrise. I usually walk to the M4 bus and take it across 110th Street to Fifth Avenue so I can start at the east end of the Harlem Meer, with the rising sun behind me. People who see me in the park with my lens and tripod often ask for tips on improving their photographs. My answer is always, "Point your shadow at your subject and use a tripod." I work my way south, shooting until around 11:00 a.m., when the sun gets too high. I then take a break until about 4:00 p.m., when the light gets good again. I like shooting in winter because I can sleep later and the sun never gets very high on the horizon, so I can pretty much photograph all day long. And, since there are no leaves on the trees it's easier to spot roosting hawks and owls.

The kind of wildlife photography I do requires highly specialized equipment. In addition to my main lens, an eleven-pound 600mm f/4 image-stabilized monster made by Canon, I usually have a 400mm f/5.6 with me, as well as two camera bodies, a flash, external power supply, and lots of extra batteries. In all I lug about forty pounds of equipment (see page 203) on a typical day.

I tell people that I don't take bird photographs—I take photographs with birds in them. This subtle distinction comes from being a photographer long before I became interested in birds. I would rather have a good, expressive photo of a common bird than a dull snapshot of a rare bird. It may sound cliché but I strive to photograph the "inner bird." I want my photos to have emotional impact, and I am happier with a good photo of a European Starling than I am with a lifeless photo of a Boreal Owl.

Unfortunately, the bird population in Central Park and in the world in general is in decline. Central Park's year-round residents like starlings and robins have increased their numbers over the past twenty years, but the neotropical songbird population has severely dropped. This decline has been greatest among the long-distance migrants such as warblers, orioles, tanagers, vireos, and buntings. These birds nest in North America's temperate woodland forests in summer and return to their wintering grounds in Central or South America or the Caribbean every fall. Their habitat is being destroyed both in North America and in their wintering grounds at an alarming rate.

Why are we so hell-bent on destroying our natural heritage? I think about this question a lot, and the only answer I can come up is that we no longer feel any emotional connection to our environment and its inhabitants. We destroy nesting areas, habitat, and other vital natural resources because we have lost the symbiosis we once had with the earth.

The late Susan Sontag wrote in *Against Interpretation* that "Ours is a culture based on excess, on overproduction; the result is a steady loss of sharpness in our sensory experience. All the conditions of modern life—its plentitude, its sheer crowdedness—conjoin to dull our sensory faculties." In fact, living in New York City, the epicenter of excess, often creates an impenetrable patina over one's emotions. It was with great joy that I watched so many demonstrators protesting the removal of a Red-tailed Hawk's nest from a building on Fifth Avenue. Many of the protesters were park regulars and avid bird watchers, but there were hundreds more who reacted to the plight of these magnificent birds and came out to show their support.

I believe, as Sontag did, that modern life dulls our emotions. If we wish to sharpen them again we must distill what really matters from the noise, crowding, and excess of modern urban life and hold it safe within ourselves. Once we reestablish that bond we can begin to act in ways that can protect and preserve our precious natural resources. I wrote this book because I feel a strong attachment to the birds I photograph. I wanted to share this connection with more people and hopefully, through my photographs, help them feel the bond I feel toward some of the smallest and most beautiful of God's creatures.

winter

Ducks. That's one of the big stories in Central Park during the winter. Moving south from their summer breeding grounds, many species of ducks find the food supply in Central Park to their liking so they stick around. During colder winters the lakes and ponds freeze and the amount of open water gets smaller and smaller so that by mid-January the ducks become concentrated in the one or two areas of open water. It is possible to get closer to certain species of ducks in Central Park's lakes in the winter than you ever could in the wild.

PRECEDING PAGES
page 12: Cardinal in snow
pages 14–15: Central Park Lake

OPPOSITE
Male Wood Duck resting on the ice in late afternoon
Central Park Lake

Female Wood Duck
Central Park Lake

Wood Ducks usually stop by the park only for a day or two, but occasionally they will stay much longer. Other winters you won't see them at all. I prefer the female Wood Duck's subtle coloration but she obviously prefers the male's striking red, green, blue, black, and tan plumage. It's no wonder they are considered one of America's most beautiful birds. Yet this extraordinary plumage is the very thing that makes the male Wood Duck tough to photograph. The graduation from dark purple to brilliant white makes it hard to hold detail in both areas. I usually overexpose the whites a little in order to bring out detail in the darker areas. The female (above) is beating her wings to remove excess water. Although duck's feathers are coated with a lanolin-like substance that allows them to shed water, most ducks, especially those that dive or "dabble" for food, need to beat the excess water from their wings before they can fly.

Pied-billed Grebe
Harlem Meer

Dabbling ducks feed by plunging their heads underwater, leaving only their tails above the surface. They take off directly from the water and are fun to photograph as they burst into flight. Geese and swans, because of their bulk, will run across the top of the water, their large webbed feet propelling them forward until they gain enough speed to take off. Grebes resemble ducks but belong to a different family. Every year several species of Grebes visit Central Park's lakes and ponds.

Male Gadwall at sunrise
Harlem Meer

Female Ruddy Duck at sunrise
Harlem Meer

Pekin Ducks mating
Harlem Meer

Pekin Ducks are large white domestic ducks. *Peking Duck* is a dish on the menu of some Chinese restaurants. The Pekin Ducks in Central Park are most likely from the live poultry market on 116th Street and Park Avenue. They can't fly, because their wings are clipped, so they must have walked (or waddled) from 116th down to the Harlem Meer at 110th Street. On the other hand they might have been bought as presents and then released in the park when they grew too large. In any case there are at least a half dozen of them in the waters of Central Park at any one time. They seem to enjoy their life in the park and are quite tame. People love to feed them, and the other ducks and geese cohabitate with them nicely. Turkeys and Ring-necked Pheasants are also seen in the park from time to time, but the Pekin Ducks have become permanent residents.

Toward the end of winter, American Woodcocks are among the first birds to show up in the park on their journey north. They are very difficult to spot because they look like the dead leaves they forage in. When threatened they will freeze and remain motionless, sometimes for hours. This photo was taken in February while there was still plenty of snow on the ground. This one was rooting around the Upper Lobe when some birders pointed him out to me.

Frequent winter visitors, Hooded Mergansers are seen on Central Park Lake, the Reservoir, and Harlem Meer. They drift in the open water, sleeping much of the day and occasionally diving for food. They are most active in early morning and late afternoon. In addition to Hooded Mergansers (the smallest in the merganser family), Common (the largest mergansers) and Red-breasted Mergansers (who usually prefer brackish water) can also be seen on Central Park's lakes.

CLOCKWISE FROM ABOVE LEFT
Male Bufflehead landing
Turtle Pond

Northern Shoveler
Harlem Meer

Female Common Merganser
Harlem Meer

Female Hooded Merganser
Harlem Meer

Many ducks that winter on Central Park's lakes either show up in breeding plumage or molt into that plumage during their stay. This set of brightly colored feathers is designed to attract females, but it also attracts bird watchers and photographers. The best locations and times for observing ducks during the winter are Central Park Lake and the Harlem Meer from January through early March. The ducks are most active in the early morning and tend to move away from shore as human and dog traffic increases.

In late winter the Canada Geese and Mute Swans begin to mate. The swans become very aggressive toward the geese, chasing them all over Central Park Lake. They know a good handout when they see one and jealously guard the prime feeding spots along the water's edge. The male geese become aggressive toward each other, trying to establish their superiority over inferiors while, at the same time, avoiding the swans. It's somewhat typical behavior for avian and human New Yorkers alike.

Mute Swan walking on the ice
Central Park Lake

Canada Goose hissing at another male goose
Central Park Lake

Red-breasted Nuthatch
Evodia Field

While Tufted Titmice and White-breasted Nuthatches are commonly seen in the park in winter, less common are Red-breasted Nuthatches. They pass through during spring and fall migrations but rarely stay the winter. This Red-breasted Nuthatch (opposite) was an exception and spent a good part of the winter in Central Park, feeding on suet at the feeders in Evodia Field.

White-breasted Nuthatch
Evodia Field feeders

Carolina Wren
North Woods

OPPOSITE
**Adult male (top) and young
male Red-winged Blackbirds**
The Ramble

I especially like to get out early with my camera after a fresh snowfall. I go looking for Northern Cardinals because I love the way the male's bright red and the female's flaming orange colors stand out in contrast against the snow. It's a challenge photographing them in snow because the camera's built-in light meter will often underexpose in order to compensate for the brightness of snow. I usually overexpose by at least a half stop under these conditions.

OPPOSITE
Male Northern Cardinal feeding
Nutter's Battery

Male Blue Jay feeding
The Ravine

Competition for food can get quite aggressive at the feeders in Evodia Field. The American Goldfinches are among the most aggressive, especially as winter progresses and the male finches start to get their bright breeding plumage back.

Pine Siskins and Common Redpolls are two of the rarer species spotted at the feeders in recent years. These types of birds are known as irruptive species since they are pushed south during winter because of a loss of the food supply on their normal wintering grounds. The nice thing about the feeders is that the birds tend to stay longer because of the abundant food supply, so if a rare species is spotted it will likely be there for three or four days, allowing infrequent visitors to the park a chance to see it.

Lloyd Spitalnik, coordinator of the Evodia Field feeder project, hanging a thistle feeder.
Evodia Field feeders

OPPOSITE
Feeding Ring-billed Gulls
Central Park Lake

The feeders in Evodia Field attract countless birds throughout the winter. Maintained by a group of dedicated volunteers who fill them weekly, the feeders offer a wide variety of tasty morsels. There's a thistle sock for smaller birds like finches, seeds for larger birds, and a couple of suet feeders for the Northern Creepers, titmice, nuthatches, and wood-peckers. I try to visit the feeders at least once a day in winter to see what's going on. I also like the feeders because the smaller birds feeding there attract larger predators. I have probably gotten more shots of hawks in the area around the feeders than in any other place in the park.

Hairy Woodpecker
The Ramble

OPPOSITE
Juvenile Red-headed Woodpecker
103rd Street and Central Park West

Red-bellied Woodpecker
The Ravine

Red-bellied Woodpeckers, Northern Flickers, and Yellow-bellied Sapsuckers are all winter residents of the park. Although Red-headed Woodpeckers pass through during migration they usually don't stay the winter. One recent winter, however, a juvenile Red-headed Woodpecker with only a bit of red on his head took up residence near 103rd Street and Central Park West. Red-headed Woodpeckers hide their food in the indentations in tree bark. This one seemed to favor pin oak acorns and liked to stash them in the deep indentions of locust trees. At one point it flew down to the sidewalk on Central Park West and took a bath in a curbside puddle as traffic whizzed by.

Yellow-bellied Sapsucker
North Woods

Female Northern Flicker
The Loch

Northern Flickers live in Central Park year-round. They breed and raise their young there and are constantly contending with starlings for nesting cavities. Brightly colored, the Northern Flicker has a bright red spot on the back of its head, and its yellow breast is speckled with black spots. The male has a black "moustache," and the undersides of both male and female wings are a bright lemon yellow.

One of the most difficult birds to spot is the Brown Creeper, who blends in perfectly with his background. I've noticed that when a hawk comes near, all the other birds fly away, but the Creeper freezes and waits for the hawk to leave, his perfect camouflage protecting him. The Brown Creeper is the only tree-climbing bird on the East Coast that starts feeding at the bottom of a tree and works its way up.

Brown Creeper
The Ramble

**Tufted Titmouse eating
an acorn**
Evodia Field

House Finch
The Pool

One reason so many species of birds spend the winter in Central Park is the abundant food supply. Nuts, berries, and seeds abound in winter and although humans supplement these it would take hundreds and hundreds of bird feeders to equal the natural bounty available in the park. There are many species of bird-edible fruit-bearing trees, and the fruit stays on the trees long after the leaves have fallen away, making it easier to spot. When we've had a particularly warm autumn, the berries stay on the trees longer than usual and eventually ferment. Birders have told me they've seen birds eating these fermented berries, becoming intoxicated, and flying around in a semi-drunken stupor.

Carolina Wren eating suet
Evodia Field feeders

Cooper's Hawk eyeing its prey
Evodia Field

Sharp-shinned Hawk
The Ramble

Pale Male is New York City's most famous hawk. Over the past ten years this Red-tailed Hawk has produced twenty-six offspring with various mates. His current mate, Lola, has been with him for several years. He gets his name from his unusual pale, almost transparent coloration. While there are several pairs of Red-tailed Hawks that nest in Central Park, Pale Male is one of the few Red-tails on record that has built his nest on a building. Red-tailed Hawks just don't do that.

The official hawk-watching season begins in January, when Pale Male and Lola return to their nest on Fifth Avenue, opposite the Model Boat Pond, and begin tidying it up. They can be seen perched in the Ramble tearing bark from trees or soaring high above the park on late afternoon thermals. Observant hawk watchers see (and hear) the pair mating in February, and by mid-March eggs have been laid. For the next thirty-five to forty days they will take turns incubating the eggs; after the eggs have hatched the pair will share parental responsibility, with one hawk staying on the nest at all times.

Thousands of people watch the two Red-tails build their nest and raise and fledge their young from a vantage point next to the Model Boat Pond. The hawks have been the subject of a PBS documentary, countless local news stories, and a charming book by Marie Winn, *Red-tails in Love*. Marie is responsible for giving Pale Male his name.

In December 2004, the board of directors of the co-op at 927 Fifth Avenue, where Pale Male and Lola had their nest, voted to remove the nest from their building. The subsequent daily demonstrations in front of the building, media coverage, and international outcry forced them to reconsider their decision. The anti-pigeon spikes that had anchored the nest, which been removed by the co-op board along with the nest, were returned, and by the first week of January 2005 the hawks were observed rebuilding their nest.

OPPOSITE
Pale Male

TOP
Emily and Nina demonstrate in support of hawks.

BOTTOM
Crowds of hawk watchers gather daily at the Model Boat Pond to scrutinize every detail of Pale Male's life.

Birds of Central Park

Birds of Central Park

Nervous squirrels are a good indication that a hawk is nearby

In winter it's possible to see quite a few different species of hawks. I was walking by the feeders in Evodia Field one clear winter's day when a Sharp-shinned Hawk flew in and perched above the feeders for a minute or two. All the birds that were feeding took off as I slowly circled around, so I had a clear shot of him with the light behind me.

I had never before seen a Red-tailed Hawk perch on a lamppost, but I guess living in New York City can make birds, as well as people, do strange things.

Often a group of crows or Blue Jays will "mob" a hawk or owl perched in a tree. They do it to drive a potential predator from the area, but I have rarely seen a mature owl or hawk succumb to this mobbing so I keep a sharp ear out for these distinctive sounds, which usually bring me to the bird.

Another way of spotting hawks is to listen for particular squirrel sounds. When a hawk is perched in a nearby tree, one or more squirrels will start what I can only describe as a pathetic mewing, which serves to warn other squirrels in the neighborhood that a predator is afoot. I usually spot the hawk nearby.

Architectural detail
Bethesda Fountain

OPPOSITE
Long-eared Owl
Bow Bridge

Long-eared Owls visit the park in the winter, but they usually roost high up in the pine trees and are nearly impossible to photograph. Recently a remarkable thing happened: Five Long-eared Owls appeared one day low in a tree near Bow Bridge. They'd sleep all day, fly out at sunset, and return before dawn. The tree was next to a major path along the edge of Central Park Lake that led to Bow Bridge so there was often a crowd of bird watchers and tourists gathered there. People didn't seem to bother the owls, but if a dog got too close one or more of them would snap awake and look down with a stare that could kill. The Long-eared Owl at right is focusing his malevolent gaze upon a dog that has just disturbed his slumber. Not far from where the owls were roosting is a pedestal decorated with an owl carving. Did Olmstead and Vaux know this would become a favorite area for visiting owls?

During the New York Audubon Society's 103rd annual Christmas Bird
Count, Jim Demes, a rare-book dealer and avid birder, discovered a
Boreal Owl in the southwest section of the park. Jim initially identified
the bird as a Saw-whet Owl, which looks very similar to a Boreal Owl,
and besides, a Boreal Owl had never before been sighted in Central Park.
Late that evening Peter Post, who has been birding in the park for over
fifty years, stopped by to see the owl and immediately recognized it as a
Boreal Owl. The owl stayed around for at least two weeks, and because it
is so rarely seen even in its normal breeding territory, birders flew in
from around the country to witness this once-in-a-lifetime event.

Boreal Owl
Tavern on the Green

spring

During the spring migration, thousands of colorful warblers move through the park on their journey back to their northern breeding grounds. The abundance of insects and other nutrient-rich food makes Central Park an ideal resting stop for these neotropical migrants, on their long and arduous trek. Since a large percentage of warbler migration takes place at night, flocks of birders can be discovered in the park at sunrise—binoculars at the ready—searching for the previous night's arrivals. During peak migration in May, it's not unusual to see a couple hundred birders on crisp spring mornings when prevailing winds have pushed migrants up from the south.

PRECEDING PAGES
Male Blackburnian Warbler
Tupelo Meadow

Female Baltimore Oriole feeding on wisteria
North Woods

Every March, around the 15th of the month, an Eastern Phoebe is spotted in the Ramble. I know that spring can't be too far off when I hear the male's familiar *fee-bee* as he returns to his breeding ground to stake out his territory. The Eastern Phoebe was the first bird ever banded in the United States. In 1804, a young John James Audubon tied a silver thread around the leg of some nestlings to see if they would come back to the same spot the next year, and sure enough, when he checked the nests a year later, there the phoebes were with silver threads around their legs.

I enjoy photographing phoebes. They are plucky little birds and I admire the way they snatch insects out of midair. Although this is a characteristic of all flycatchers, phoebes seem to do it with an extra bit of style. They will sit near the tip of a branch wagging their tails and watching for insects. All of a sudden they'll pounce, and a split second later they are back on the same branch having swallowed the insect whole. In the shot at right, the phoebe is diving from a branch hanging over the Pool, at 103rd Street. It took me a couple of hours and forty to fifty shots before I got the one I wanted.

Eastern Phoebe
The Pool

Northern Waterthrush
foraging for food
The Loch

Yellow-rumped Warbler
Nutter's Battery

**Female Black-and-white
Warbler**
The Ravine

OPPOSITE
Male Black-and-white Warbler
The Ravine

Ovenbird
The Ravine

Worm-eating Warbler
The Ravine

Pine Warbler
Nutter's Battery

OPPOSITE
Palm Warbler
Nutter's Battery

Pine and Palm Warblers are among the first warblers to arrive in the park in spring. Their subdued coloration reflects the fact that the park still wears its drab winter coat. In order to survive during their early migration, these birds must blend in with their surroundings. The reddish brown cap on the Palm Warbler is almost an exact match for many of the buds forming on the trees where it searches for early spring insects.

Prairie Warbler
The Ravine

Prairie Warbler snatching up an insect
Nutter's Battery

Prairie Warblers show up in the park in early spring but not as early as their cousins, the Pine and Palm Warblers. Like many warblers, the male is brightly colored: yellow below with black streaks and face stripes. Mature males show a hint of chestnut coloration on their olive yellow backs. They are smallish, hardworking insect eaters that are easy to spot from below because of their bright colors and constantly wagging tails. Like Pine and Palm Warblers, they tend to stay low in trees and bushes and are, therefore, much easier to photograph. The hardest part of getting a good shot of a Prairie Warbler (or any other warbler, for that matter) is that they are small and fast. When shooting warblers I set my Canon 1D on continuous-shooting mode. I also use a 1.4 converter on my 600mm f/4 lens to bring these tiny birds closer. When the bird is close enough I fire off five to six shots in a row. Usually that's all the time I have before the bird is off to another branch looking for food.

The Magnolia Warbler is one of the more common warblers in Central Park. This lovely little bird, like many of its brethren, has an inappropriate name, which was given to it when a flock was first discovered in a stand of magnolia trees. In fact, this species prefers spruce and pine, and breeds in the boreal forests of Canada. "Maggies" feed on insects found on the undersides of leaves and I have seen them perform some amazing acrobatics in search of food. Because they tend to spread their tail while foraging, one quick way to identify them is by the broad white stripe on their black tails, seen only when the tail is open. No other warbler has these white patches—visible even in its nonbreeding plumage—on its tail.

LEFT
Magnolia Warbler
Tanner's Spring

ABOVE
Magnolia Warbler singing
The Ravine

New York City's former mayor Ed Koch once said,
"Sometimes you eat the bear and sometimes the bear eats
you." That sentiment applies to photographing warblers.
Although most of the time you only get a fleeting glimpse
of these birds, sometimes a warbler will suddenly appear
in front of you and allow you to take his picture. On this
particular occasion, a beautiful male Hooded Warbler
popped up and perched on a branch about twenty feet
away from me. He let me photograph him for at least
two minutes—a long time in warbler time—and then
he was gone. I have never since gotten this close to a
Hooded Warbler.

Hooded Warbler
The Ravine

This male Common Yellowthroat looks very similar to the Hooded Warbler. All of the yellow-black warblers were terribly confusing to me when I first started out. I usually just took their picture and tried to identify them later. After several years of this, I finally have the ability to recognize a bird as I am snapping its picture.

The shot of the Yellow Warbler sitting on the fence (page 83) was taken seconds after the photo at right. After the Common Yellowthroat flew off I turned around and there behind me was this wonderful bird. It was misty, and the yellow jumped out against the rain-soaked grass. Too often, when photographing difficult subjects like warblers, the tendency is to relax after you get the shot. I have taken so many great shots immediately after I took what I thought was "the shot" that I always look around, just in case.

Male Common Yellowthroat
Turtle Pond

Yellow Warbler
Turtle Pond

Male Mourning Warbler
Tupelo Meadow

OPPOSITE
Female Canada Warbler
The Ravine

Some birds are quite cooperative—tame, almost. This Mourning Warbler was one of those. He stuck around for over a week feeding low in the grass near a large tupelo tree. Although he was hard to photograph down in the grass, every once in a while he would fly up to a low-hanging branch and remain there for a second or two. Of the two days I spent photographing him this is the only usable shot I got. Like other strangely named warblers, this bird gets its name from the black patch on its breast—supposedly a sign of mourning. This bird is often heard before it is seen. In fact, many birders have told me they often hear a Mourning Warbler without actually seeing it.

The Canada Warbler at right is probably a female. Her yellowish color is duller and her necklace is quite washed-out. This warbler got its name by virtue of being discovered in Canada, although its range is by no means limited to that country.

Bay-breasted Warbler
The Ravine

The Bay-breasted Warbler is one of our larger warblers. These handsome birds winter in northern South America and Panama and move north to breed in the boreal forests of Canada. The Bay-breasted Warbler does not dart about from limb to limb like its smaller relatives. It will spend a fair amount of time feeding in one area. The photographs of both the Bay-breasted Warbler and the Northern Parula were taken in the same spot but on different days. I have several spots I stake out during spring migration. They are mostly in the Ravine or North Woods, where there are fewer birders, pedestrians, and unleashed dogs.

Northern Parula
The Ravine

Male Blackpoll Warbler
The Point

Female Blackpoll Warbler
Tanner's Spring

TOP
**Female (left) and male
American Redstarts**
The Ravine

BOTTOM
**Female (left) and male
Blackburnian Warblers**
The Ravine

Female (left) and male
Indigo Buntings
The Ravine

I marvel at how different male and female plumage is in certain species. Many male warblers are splendidly plumed while the females appear dull and drab. This is called sexual dimorphism and is a result of natural selection: In order to attract a suitable female and induce her to breed, a male must prove his superiority over other males. Brighter plumage, as far as the female is concerned, means the male is healthy and strong and will make an ideal mate. In fact, some scientists feel there is a direct correlation between brightness of plumage and parasite levels. In other words, the brighter the plumage the fewer parasites the bird has and therefore the healthier his genes. The female, on the other hand, has to sit on the nest and incubate the eggs. There's no advantage to her being brightly colored: She needs to blend in with her surroundings so she can protect the nest and its occupants.

Male Baltimore Oriole
North Woods

Male Scarlet Tanager
North Woods

Juvenile Summer Tanager
North Woods

I rely on a group of Central Park regulars to help me find birds. This juvenile Summer Tanager (fairly rare for the park) was spotted by several people birding in the north end one early spring morning. While birders will usually observe a bird for a minute or two and move on, I will often stay in one place for over an hour if conditions are right. For the shot above I went to the spot where the bird had been seen, but it wasn't there. After waiting about an hour and a half, the bird returned and perched in a tree about thirty feet away. I snapped away for at least five minutes before he took off.

**Male House Sparrow with nest
material in his beak**
Great Lawn

By mid- to late spring the birds that are going to breed in Central Park
are well on their way to building their nests. House Sparrows seem to
favor the lampposts of Central Park. I suppose good nesting spaces, like
apartments, are in short supply.

Nest in a lamppost
Great Lawn

OPPOSITE
A Baltimore Oriole nest held together with monofilament
The Pool

This Red-bellied Woodpecker is cleaning out the debris left over from his nest-building activities.
The Ramble

**Red-tailed Hawk chicks
in their nest**
Fifth Avenue

These two Red-tailed Hawk chicks, the offspring of Pale Male and Lola, are
looking for their sibling who was just blown out of the nest while flapping
his wings. Although his first flight was inadvertent, the young hawk made it
to the top of the Fifth Avenue building where his nest is located. All three
chicks eventually fledged but remained in the area while being fed and
trained to hunt by their parents. During the summer it's not unusual to see
Pale Male and Lola's offspring around the Model Boat Pond, sitting on
branches fifteen to twenty feet up. This shot was taken from the balcony of
a fifteenth-floor apartment in an adjacent building owned by Dr. Alexander
Fisher. Dr. Fisher was an avid member of the hawk-watching community
who was kind enough to let me photograph from his balcony on numerous
occasions. Dr. Fisher passed away in July of 2004, just a few weeks shy of his
ninety-ninth birthday. He will be missed.

House Wren at a wren box
Wildflower Meadow

Although Cedar Waxwings move through the park in spring and fall they rarely nest there. This nest was hidden way up in a tree near the Shakespeare Garden and was pointed out to me by a pair of passionate birders, Howard and Anita Stillman. I never would have found it without their help. I had to put a 2X teleconverter on my 600mm lens in order to get this shot of the mother incubating her eggs.

OPPOSITE
Cedar Waxwing
Shakespeare Garden

**Female Northern Flicker
incubating her eggs**
Central Park Lake

summer

Birds of Central Park

The long days of summer bring herons, egrets, and cormorants to Central Park's lakes and streams. The fishing is good throughout the summer, and in mid-August there is a run on crayfish—a delicacy prized by egrets and herons alike.

Summer is nesting season for birds that breed in the park. In addition to robins, starlings, grackles, and Northern Flickers, I have recently observed and photographed Wood Thrushes and Cedar Waxwings building nests and raising their young in the park.

PRECEDING PAGES
**Great Blue Heron
with a crayfish**
The Pool

Bow Bridge

One summer, robins built their nest in the statue of Romeo and Juliet that stands in front of the Delacorte Theatre near the Great Lawn—one of the busiest areas of the park. Mother and chicks seem to be contemplating Romeo as he bends over to plant a kiss on Juliet. Perhaps this romantic inclination is the reason robins breed so prolifically in the park, often having a second and sometimes a third brood in the same summer.

Robin and her chicks
Delacorte Theatre

OPPOSITE
Northern Flicker feeding young
Central Park West Drive

Baltimore Oriole chick takes its first flight
North Woods

**A Wood Thrush chick begs
for food as an older sibling
looks on**
The Ramble

**Green Heron chicks
waiting to be fed**
The Upper Lobe

OPPOSITE
Green Heron chick being fed
The Upper Lobe

Every year, Green Herons nest in the Upper Lobe, delivering at least one brood and sometimes two in a season. I have, on many mornings, set my camera up on the opposite side of the Lobe from the nests and spent all morning photographing the young herons. The eggs take two to three weeks to incubate, during which time the parents take turns sitting on the nest. After they hatch, the chicks take another four to five weeks to fledge. As the chicks mature, the simple ritual of feeding turns into a brawl. The parents dutifully bring a gullet full of predigested fish to the nest, and the chicks fight for the first morsel. In the photo at right a parent is regurgitating a fish into the chick's mouth.

This Eastern Kingbird parent has just snatched an Eastern Amberwing Dragonfly from the air and is feeding it to the chick. As the chicks mature, the parent will start returning with food to the general area of the nest rather than to the nest itself. The hungry chick is forced to leave the nest and will hop from limb to limb to get to the food. Eventually that hopping will turn into flying, and the chick will fledge.

In a 1998 nesting-bird census of Central Park sponsored by New York City Audubon, over thirty-one species were reported nesting in the park that summer. While this count included birds that do well living in close proximity to humans (starlings, robins, grackles, sparrows, etc.) there were species not usually found nesting in the park, including Great Crested Flycatchers, Baltimore Orioles, Cedar Waxwings, and Wood Thrushes. During a recent summer I observed a pair of Wood Thrushes build two separate nests and raise two broods in the Ramble simultaneously. The Wood Thrushes exhibited a high degree of creativity in weaving bits and pieces of man-made items into their nests: Both nests were quite heavily festooned with toilet paper.

OPPOSITE
Eastern Kingbird feeding young
The Pool

**Female Mallard and
her ducklings**
Turtle Pond

Canada Geese goslings
Turtle Pond

Black-crowned Night Herons arrive at the Harlem Meer in early spring and are well-known to the local fishermen who often catch and release their fish on the ground near a waiting Night Heron. The herons are quite acclimated to the dogs and people that frequent the Meer and can often be seen perched on rocks that jut out into the western end, or sitting in the trees that line the lake—usually close to a fisherman who is having good luck. On page 125, a Night Heron, nicknamed Ralph, is sprinting off with his latest prize.

Black-crowned Night Heron
Harlem Meer

PRECEDING PAGES, LEFT
Great Egret
Harlem Meer

PRECEDING PAGES, RIGHT
**Black-crowned Night Heron
ignoring the catch-and-release
rule**
Harlem Meer

OPPOSITE
Great Egret in flight at sunrise
Harlem Meer

Snowy Egret at dawn
Harlem Meer

Turtle Pond gets its name from the large number of turtles living there. Although there is at least one Snapping Turtle that calls the pond home, all the rest of the turtles are Red-eared Sliders, the most common variety sold in pet stores. The observation deck at Turtle Pond is one of the best places in the park to get close to nature and to photograph ducks, geese, herons, and, yes, turtles.

OPPOSITE
Great Egret perched on the observation deck
Turtle Pond

Double-crested Cormorant drying its wings
Turtle Pond

Over the course of several days one recent spring, I was rewarded with some incredible views of Snowy Egrets fishing and preening. These Snowies, as they are called, that normally fly over the Meer but never land, stayed for five days, arriving before dawn and flying off when too many people and dogs had arrived. These photographs (pages 127 and 131) may be some of the only shots ever taken of Snowy Egrets in Central Park.

Snowy Egret
Harlem Meer

**A Black-crowned Night Heron
goes over park rules with a
group of recently arrived Pekin
Ducks**
Harlem Meer

A Ring-billed Gull enjoying a nosh
Central Park Lake

Canada Goose
Harlem Meer

The Harlem Meer is one of two places where catch-and-release fishing is allowed in Central Park. The other is Central Park Lake. There are quite a few regulars, including Ken (right), one of the best fishermen around and someone who is generous with his knowledge. Ken is quite protective of the Meer and its nonhuman residents. Here he is petting Quackers, a remarkably tame Mallard that will allow certain people pick it up and carry it around.

Mallard and friend
Harlem Meer

OPPOSITE
A Red-winged Blackbird being hand-fed by a Turtle Pond regular in the rain

A Red-winged Blackbird chasing a Great Egret that came too close to its nest
Turtle Pond

There are two variations of the Eastern Screech Owl: Gray Morph and Rufous Morph. The owl below is a rufous morph, so named because of its foxy-red coloration. The bird at right is a Gray Morph. When I was shooting the owl at right it was being mobbed by crows and voicing its disapproval. Eastern Screech Owls nested in the park until the 1960s when their decline and disappearance was attributed to poisons used in rodent control. In 1997 two dozen screech owls were released into the park by Urban Park Rangers. These are two of the few remaining. No one knows what happened to the others, but, until recently there continued to be sightings of at least one owl.

Eastern Screech Owl
Central Park Lake

OPPOSITE
Eastern Screech Owl
Warbler Rock

The Common Grackle is one of the most abundant
breeding birds in Central Park. This large black, iridescent
bird with yellow eyes is an omnivore, switching from plants
to small vertebrates and insects as the need arises. Like
most birds, grackles launch themselves into the air before
they begin flapping their wings. I captured the shot above
at the exact moment this grackle jumped off his perch.

Eastern Kingbird
Nutter's Battery

Fresh water is essential to the survival of most birds. Whether for drinking, bathing, or just cooling off, fresh water sources abound in Central Park, including several natural springs. One of the most popular bathing spots I have run across is the small creek that runs through the Ravine. I have taken literally hundreds of pictures of birds bathing and preening there, everything from tiny warblers to Red-tailed Hawks. Another favorite bathing spot is Tanner's Spring, near the West Eighty-first Street entrance to the park.

Northern Cardinal searching for water
Nutter's Battery

Nearly every species of bird has been observed bathing. Some, like House Sparrows, stand at the edge of the water and just splash around, while others like robins, Blue Jays, and most warblers get deeper into the water, completely submerging themselves. After bathing, birds preen. Preening returns feathers to their correct position so that flight is possible, and often involves the addition of oil to the feathers from the uropygial gland, usually located near the rear of the bird. The oil from this gland helps keep feathers flexible, fights parasites, and in some species provides waterproofing. A bird will use its bill to "nibble" along the edges of feathers to spread the oil while at the same time rooting out mites and straightening the feathers so that barbs interlock again and flight can occur.

Magnolia Warbler
The Ravine

OPPOSITE, CLOCKWISE FROM
TOP LEFT
Northern Flicker
The Ravine

Blue Jay
The Ravine

American Robin
The Ravine

**Juvenile Red-tailed Hawk
preening**
Belvedere Castle

OPPOSITE
Gray Catbird preening
The Ravine

Ruby-throated Hummingbird
Shakespeare Garden

Ruby-throated Hummingbird
Shakespeare Garden

The eastern United States is home to only one native species of hummingbird: the Ruby-throated Hummingbird. These tiny birds, measuring
three to four inches from beak to tail, move through the park in spring
and late summer as they migrate to and from their wintering grounds in
Central America. Their migration coincides with the flowering of certain
key plant species along their route. Ruby-throated Hummingbirds are
especially fond of the several species of salvia found in Central Park's
Shakespeare Garden.

Mallards and Red-eared Sliders are common in the lakes and ponds of Central Park. They often share sunny spots, but this is the first time I have ever seen a Mallard take an interest in a turtle.

Mallard
Harlem Meer

August is a relatively quiet month in the park as many New Yorkers leave the city for their summer houses or for more extended vacations to other parts of the country and globe. As jewelweed begins to flower in early September, Ruby-throated Hummingbirds start appearing. Darting quickly from flower to flower, they are extremely difficult to photograph but well worth the effort. Some years, summerlike weather continues well into late October, and many migrants linger in the park, taking their time preparing for the long journey south.

Mallard at sunset
Turtle Pond

fall

Fall is migration time and many species of migratory birds stop in Central Park. On some unusually cool mornings I've found hundreds of warblers and other nocturnal migrants in the park, pushed southward by a cold front that moved through the area during the night.

The fishing is still good in September and October, so long-legged waders like egrets and herons continue to feed. Great Blue Herons will stay well into November or even December, if mild weather prevails.

PRECEDING PAGES
Cedar Waxwing
The Pool

Turtle Pond as seen from Belvedere Castle

Birds of Central Park

OPPOSITE
**A Great Egret on a successful
late-afternoon fishing
expedition**
Central Park Lake

Great Blue Heron in light snow
Turtle Pond

Double-crested Cormorant
Harlem Meer

Spotted Sandpiper
The Pool

**Milkweed seedpod
bursting open**
Wildflower Meadow

OPPOSITE
Eastern Phoebe
The Pool

Eastern Phoebes will stick around as long as there are
insects to eat. They are usually gone by late October but
will be back in early March. In the fall their breasts turn
a pale yellow, blending nicely with the fall foliage.

**Ruby-crowned Kinglet feeding
on ragweed**
Wildflower Meadow

Gray Catbird
Green Bench

The abundance of fruit-bearing trees makes the park a very popular spot with fruit-eating species such as Cedar Waxwings and thrushes. Juneberries, hackberries, crab apples, hawthorn, and many other types of fruit-bearing trees can be found in all areas of the park. In the fall, flocks of Cedar Waxwings will move through the park, eating their way from the north to south end. There are several trees near the Pool at 103rd Street that I stake out in October and early November in the late afternoon, when the sun is behind me. I usually get a decent shot or two like this one of a male and female Cedar Waxwing feasting on hackberries.

Cedar Waxwings
The Pool

Just a few months ago these warblers, brightly colored harbingers of spring, passed through Central Park on their way to their northern breeding grounds. Returning on their southward journey most warblers have shed their conspicuous plumage in favor of something drabber. No need to impress a female now, so why draw attention—just head south and make sure you don't get snapped up by a migrating raptor. Also moving south is the summer's crop of newborns, their dull first-year plumage adding to the confusion. Most field guides have a section called "Confusing Fall Warblers," but in many cases it's extremely difficult to make a precise identification as to sex and age.

Palm Warbler
Wildflower Meadow

Blackpoll Warbler
Shakespeare Garden

Black-throated Green Warbler
The Ravine

**Magnolia Warbler feeding on
the undersides of leaves**
Belvedere Castle

Wilson's Warbler
Great Hill

Chestnut-sided Warbler
Great Hill

Palm Warbler
Shakespeare Garden

Brown Thrasher
Great Hill

OPPOSITE
Swainson's Thrush
Green Bench

OPPOSITE
Hermit Thrush
Wildflower Meadow

**Eastern Bluebird,
the official New York
State bird**
The Pool

The strange little bird at left appeared one fall day at the Pool while I was photographing Cedar Waxwings feeding at a fruit tree. I took quite a few shots but could not make an identification. Lloyd Spitalnik, one of the most discerning birders I know, identified it as a leucistic Ruby-crowned Kinglet. Leucism is a condition where normal plumage appears very pale as a result of weak pigmentation. It is similar to albinism (a total lack of pigmentation) and is genetic, not environmental.

House Sparrow
Turtle Pond

The House Sparrow is one of the most common birds found in America. It has been estimated that there are twice as many House Sparrows in the park as all other native songbird species combined—an amazing statistic when you consider the House Sparrow is not native to North America. The House Sparrow is an Old World sparrow originating in Europe. Also known as an English Sparrow it was first brought to the United States in the mid-1850s to combat an inchworm infestation that was decimating Central Park's trees. The first pairs didn't survive the harsh New England winters but more were brought over and eventually they took hold. Over the next twenty-five years the birds spread rapidly across the country, destroying crops and pushing out native songbirds.

House Sparrows
Bow Bridge

White-throated Sparrow
Great Hill

Swamp Sparrow
Wildflower Meadow

Song Sparrow
The Pool

Field Sparrow
The Pool

American Goldfinch
Wildflower Meadow

OPPOSITE
Purple Finch
Conservatory Garden

European Starlings were brought to this country in a similar manner to House Sparrows. In the 1890s, a New York City resident dedicated to introducing all the birds mentioned in Shakespeare's works into Central Park introduced European Starlings. Today, flocks of hundreds of thousands of these starlings are a common sight across most of the United States. Not only do starlings compete for food with native species, they are adept at stealing nest cavities from woodpeckers and other tree-cavity nesters. A starling will literally wait for a flicker or woodpecker to finish hollowing out its nest in a dead tree and then move in and take over. Both starlings and House Sparrows thrive on bread crumbs and other scraps left by humans and are well suited for survival in an urban environment.

European Starling
Near the Reservoir

**Northern Flicker flicking
his tongue**
Green Bench

OPPOSITE
**Male Northern Cardinal
eating termites**
Willow Rock

In spring, termite hatch-outs are exciting events because they whip insect-eating birds into feeding frenzies. Oblivious to humans, the birds will gorge themselves on the newly hatched termites. I had never seen a hatch-out until I was photographing near Willow Rock one fall, and I happened to look over and see a small boulder covered with crawling insects. Hatch-outs in fall are very rare. Several Northern Cardinals moved in for a feast, but their beaks are not really designed for this sort of thing and it was very difficult for them to grab the moving termites on the hardened rock surface. To my amazement, they started using their tails to scoop the insects onto their wings so they could eat them off the soft wing surface. This went on for quite some time and, although I saw several warblers in the area, none turned up to partake in the feast.

Although Northern Flickers prefer insects, in the fall they will feed on the ripe fruit of trees. The flicker above had just enjoyed a crab apple snack and was using his long tongue, normally reserved for digging insects out of their holes, to clean off the outer edges of his beak.

Male Belted Kingfisher
The Pool

OPPOSITE
Rock Pigeons
Turtle Pond

Female Rufous Hummingbird
Strawberry Fields

The Rufous Hummingbird is native to northern California, Oregon, and Washington and is probably one of the hardiest hummingbirds in the United States. Every year a few show up in the East although this is the first confirmed sighting of this bird in Central Park. I was able to take a shot of the hummingbird above with its tail feathers spread, which is the only definitive way to identify it. The female Rufous Hummingbird lingered in and around Strawberry Fields for at least ten days in late November before moving on.

Rufous (or Allen's) Hummingbird
Conservatory Garden

As fall progresses and the days get shorter, I often find myself shooting at sunset or in the twilight that follows. This is one of my favorite times to shoot because it is often crisp and clear and the light casts a glow that lends an air of mystery to the park. Like many photographers I shoot the light, not the subject. Many an uninspired subject has been transformed by just the right lighting conditions.

**The Loeb Boathouse
at moonrise**
Central Park Lake

EQUIPMENT

I use Canon cameras and lenses exclusively. Canon's
large image-stabilized lenses make a difference
when photographing birds in the wild. Below is a
list of the typical gear I carry with me in the park.
I carry it all in a backpack and tripod bag. See my
Web site (www.calvorn.com/workflow.htm) for
details about my workflow.

① Canon 600mm f/4 image stabilized lens
   Canon 400mm f/5.6 lens
   Canon 50mm f/1.8 lens
② Canon 1D Mark II digital camera
   Canon 10D digital camera with
      external battery grip
③ Canon 1.4X teleconverter
   Canon 2X teleconverter
④ Canon 550EX flash
⑤ Canon off-camera shoe cord
⑥ Quantum 2 x 2 external battery
      for flash and camera
   Cord for flash to battery
   Cord for 1D to battery
⑦ Better Beamer flash extender
⑧ Wimberley tripod head and Gitzo self-leveling
      tripod head
⑨ Wimberley flash bracket
⑩ Gitzo carbon fiber tripod

   Really Right Stuff Arca Swiss-type quick-release
      plate for each lens
   Drop-in polarizer for the 600mm lens

   Lens cleaning kit
   Tool kit
   Firstaid kit
   Microfiber cloth
   Two extra batteries for 1D
   Two extra batteries for 10D

INDEX

ACKNOWLEDGMENTS

I WOULD LIKE TO THANK Katherine Dillon and Kate Thompson of DillonThompson Design for their unflagging faith. Without them there would be no *Birds of Central Park* and I am eternally grateful.

My friend and colleague Jeffrey Tuchman deserves special thanks. Jeff was the first person who recognized I might have a talent for wildlife photography, and his encouragement and support over the past three years have meant a great deal to me.

I would also like to thank Lloyd Spitalnik, one of the wisest and most knowledgeable birders I know for sharing his knowledge so freely with me and for his tireless efforts in checking my facts and bird identifications. Any errors that may have crept into the book are mine and mine alone and in no way reflect on Lloyd.

Arthur Morris deserves special mention. He first recognized my talent for wildlife photography and his encouragement and advice set my feet down on the right path.

Thanks also to Karen Fung, outstanding photographer and friend, for sharing her time and talent and to Terry Clarke for his keen insights into birds and birding. Also deserving of thanks is James Galetto, one of the finest wildlife photographers I know. I spent many hours photographing birds with Jimmy and I learned a great deal from him.

Tom Fiore, whose tireless efforts in finding and reporting birds in Central Park are truly Herculean, deserves special mention. Tom is also one of the most knowledgable bird and butterfly observers in the park, and I am profoundly grateful for the knowledge he has shared with me.

A special thanks goes to Marie Winn for graciously agreeing to write the foreword to this book. Marie's tireless efforts on behalf of Pale Male and Lola and Central Park earn her a special place in the hearts of all.

Author and naturalist David Rosane is responsible for the idea that germinated into this book. I am very grateful to him for his time, effort, and, most of all, his friendship.

I would like to thank other Central Park regulars for sharing their knowledge of birds and bird sightings. Among these (in alphabetical order) are: Ben Cacace, Sylvia Cohen, Rebekah Creshkoff, Jim Demes, Mike Freeman, Dick Gershon, Brian Hart, Phil Jeffrey, Lincoln Karim, Art LeMoine, Brian McPhillips, Alan Messer, Jack Meyer, Dorothy Poole, Peter Post, Brian St. Clair, Starr Sapphire, Ann Shanahan, Marty Sohmer, David Speiser, Howard and Anita Spellman, Lee Stinchcomb, Nick Wagerik, and Elliott Zichlinsky. Regina Alvarez, Central Park's Woodlands Supervisor, also deserves special mention for her extraordinary work in caring for the park's plant life.

Neil Calvanese, chief of operations for Central Park, deserves special recognition for his tireless efforts on behalf of the park and its inhabitants and for his help in providing access to various restricted areas of the park.

Editor: Andrea Danese
Designer: Dillon | Thompson
Production Manager: Jane Searle

Page 1: Great Egret, Bethesda Fountain
Page 2: Red-tailed Hawks cavorting over Central Park Lake
Page 4–5: View from Central Park looking toward the Upper
West Side

Library of Congress Cataloging-in-Publication Data
Vornberger, Cal.
Birds of Central Park / text and photography by Cal Vornberger;
foreword by Marie Winn.
p. cm.
Includes bibliographical references.
ISBN 0–8109–5917–8 (alk. paper)
1. Birds—New York (State)—New York. 2. Birds—New York
(State)—New York—Pictorial works. I. Title.
QL684.N7V67 2005
598'.09747'1—dc22
2005005863

Printed and bound in Singapore

10 9 8 7 6 5 4 3 2

Harry N. Abrams, Inc.
115 West 18th Street
New York, N.Y. 10011
www.abramsbooks.com

Abrams is a subsidiary of

LA MARTINIÈRE
GROUPE

I would also like to thank Doug Blonsky and the Central Park Conservancy for their active support of this book. Without the Conservancy's efforts Central Park would not be the wonderful place it is today.

Thanks to Andrea Danese, my editor at Abrams, and to Abrams president and CEO, Michael Jacobs, for their help in bringing this book to the world. Thanks also to my agent, Elizabeth Wales. Her efforts on behalf of *Birds of Central Park* are truly appreciated.

To E.J. McAdams, executive director of New York City Audubon, and all who participated in the rallies and demonstrations to have Pale Male and Lola's nest reinstated, a heartfelt thank you for all your efforts.

I am especially grateful to John DiMauro and the crew at Canon's Eastern Regional Factory Service in Jamesburg, New Jersey, for their efforts in keeping my equipment in top condition.

Finally, I'd like to thank Charles Kennedy. Charles, who left this world (and Central Park) a much better place than he found it, was a shining beacon for all who frequented the park. He will be missed by all who knew and loved him.

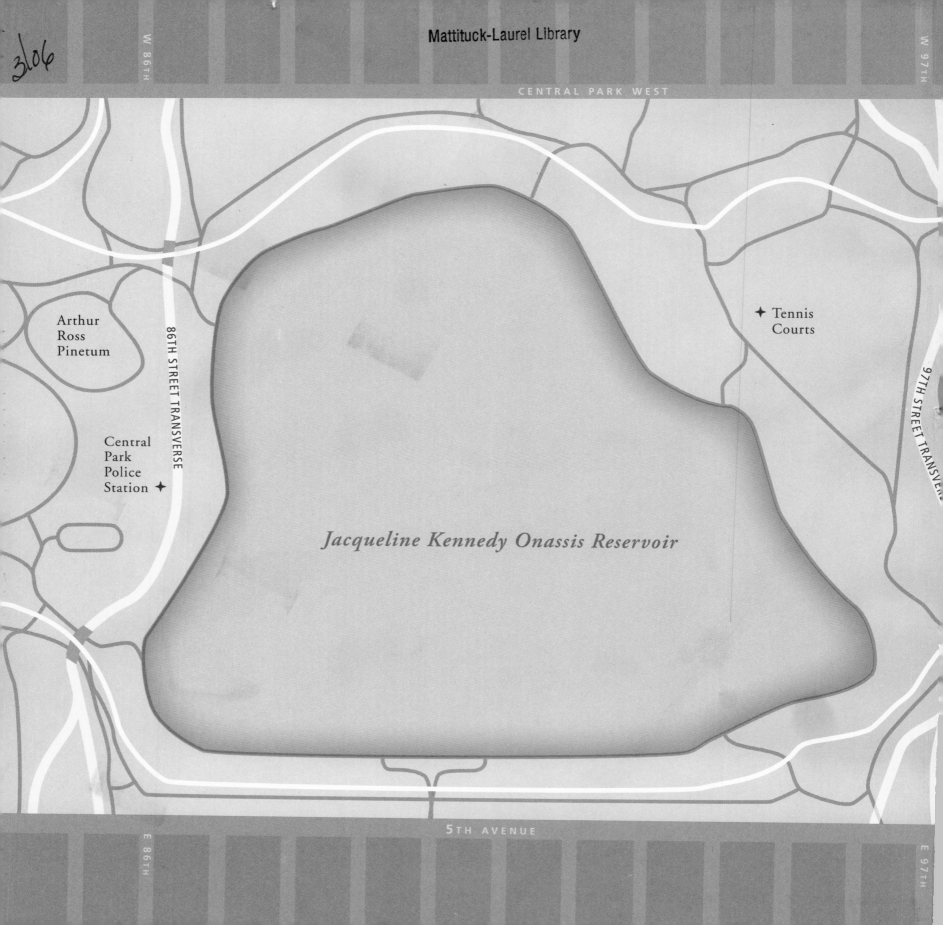

Turn the next two pages and see
life-sized portraits of two turkeys.

ALL ABOUT TURKEYS

Jim Arnosky

Scholastic Press / New York

For Susan,
who watches wild turkeys
throughout the year.

Have you ever wondered
about turkeys?
Where are wild turkeys found
and how do they live?
What do turkeys eat?
Where do they sleep?
How big can a wild turkey grow?

This book answers these questions
about turkeys and more.
It is all about turkeys.

Turkeys are big, strong, hardy birds. Wild turkeys are very wary. They may be the most wary of all birds.

Most of the time you see wild turkeys they
are away, in the distance. You can only see
their dark shapes as they move or feed.

Female turkey

Male turkey

beard

When seen much closer, those dark shapes become iridescent and shine bronze, red, and blue in the sunlight.

Male turkeys, called toms, are larger than female turkeys, which are called hens. The males are more deeply colored than the females, and are more apt to have a beard than the females. Turkey beards grow from the base of the throat and hang straight down.

Turkeys that live in desert regions are more tan in color than woodland turkeys.

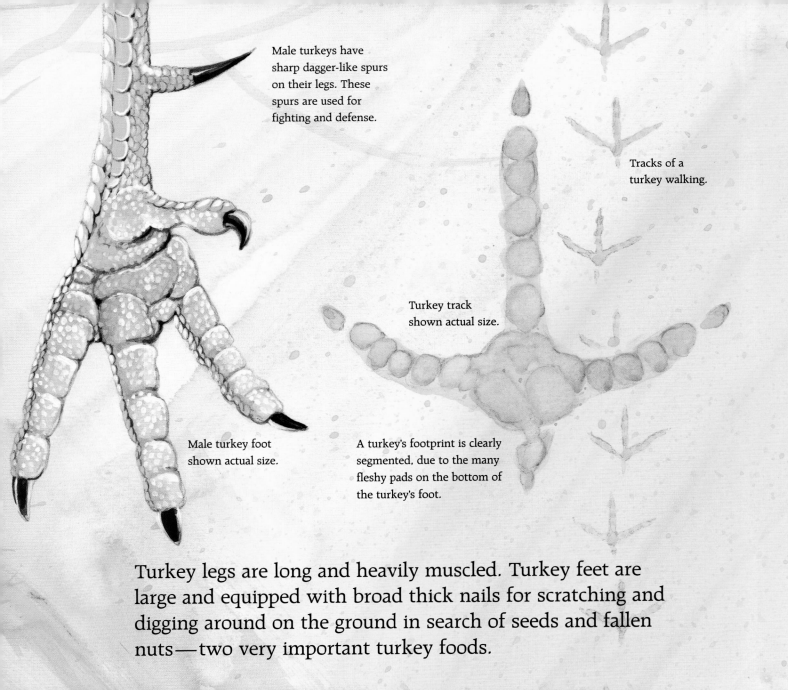

Male turkeys have sharp dagger-like spurs on their legs. These spurs are used for fighting and defense.

Tracks of a turkey walking.

Turkey track shown actual size.

Male turkey foot shown actual size.

A turkey's footprint is clearly segmented, due to the many fleshy pads on the bottom of the turkey's foot.

Turkey legs are long and heavily muscled. Turkey feet are large and equipped with broad thick nails for scratching and digging around on the ground in search of seeds and fallen nuts—two very important turkey foods.

The weird-looking protrusion on a turkey's head is called the caruncle. When a turkey is agitated, its caruncle will extend and hang over the face or beak.

A turkey has no feathers on its head, only a scattering of short hairs. This is what one male turkey's head looked like to me as seen enlarged through my telephoto lens.

Silhouette shows actual size turkey head and neck.

The fleshy folds of skin under a turkey's chin are called the wattles.

The head's ability to change color is most evident and more vibrant in males. A complete change from dull to brilliant can occur in less than a minute.
The two portraits on these pages show the same bird in only a minute's difference.

Each turkey eye has a broad monocular view. Because the eyes can look forward together, a turkey has binocular (3-dimensional) vision as well.

The head and throat of a turkey can change color from an overall gray or violet, when the bird is calm, to tri-colored red, white, and blue. The tri-coloring happens when the turkey is excited or agitated.

How well a turkey can smell is unknown. A turkey's hearing is excellent. Its eyesight, incredible! Turkeys can see the smallest, slightest movement a hundred yards away.

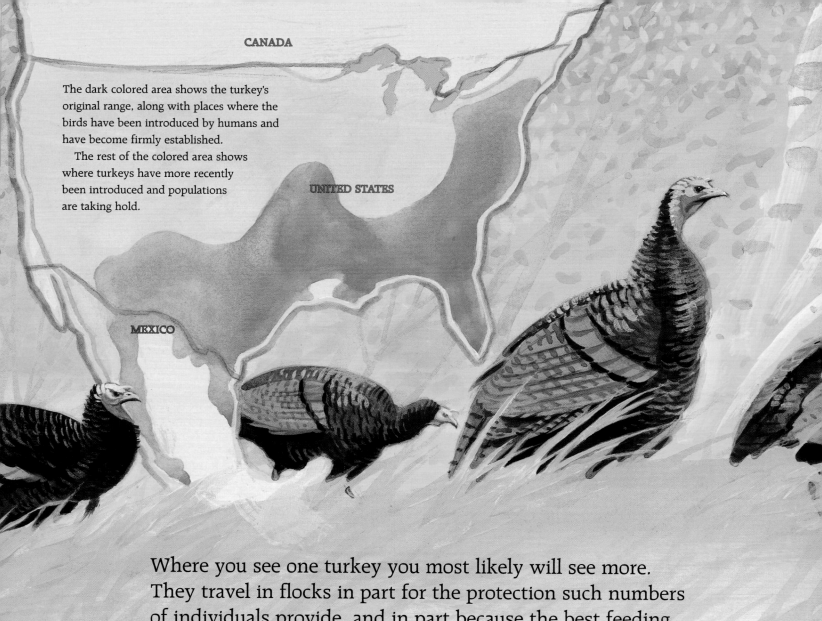

The dark colored area shows the turkey's original range, along with places where the birds have been introduced by humans and have become firmly established.

The rest of the colored area shows where turkeys have more recently been introduced and populations are taking hold.

CANADA

UNITED STATES

MEXICO

Where you see one turkey you most likely will see more. They travel in flocks in part for the protection such numbers of individuals provide, and in part because the best feeding and hiding places draw them together.

Turkeys are animals of edge lands—wherever field meets woods, or brush borders open plain. On these edges they find and eat nuts, seeds, grains, berries, greens, and any insects they can catch. In farm country, turkeys frequent cornfields after harvest when leftover kernels of corn remain scattered over the ground.

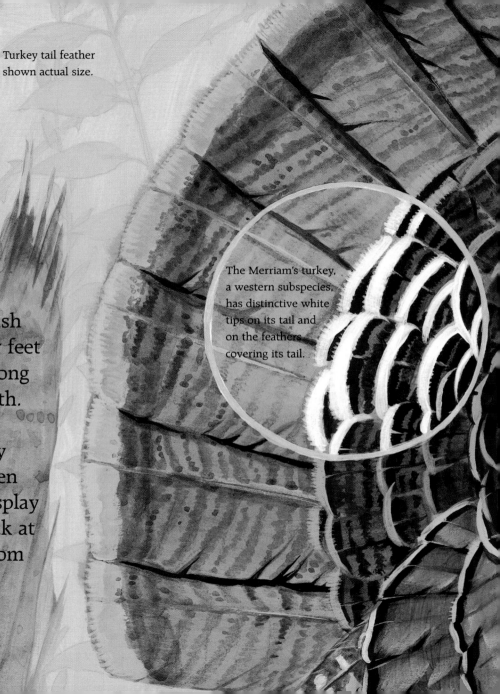

Adult male turkeys are sometimes called gobblers after the loud gobbling sound they make when proclaiming their dominance. Two gobblers claiming the same territory almost always results in vicious fighting. The combatants lash out at each other with their feet and sharp spurs. Fights among gobblers often end in a death.

During breeding season, which is late winter or early spring, gobblers become even more ill-tempered. They display their feathers and will attack at the slightest provocation from another gobbler.

Turkey tail feather shown actual size.

The Merriam's turkey, a western subspecies, has distinctive white tips on its tail and on the feathers covering its tail.

When a gobbler displays its tail feathers, its head colors deepen. Its wattles swell, and its caruncle lengthens.

The hen turkey makes her nest in a quiet, secluded, secret place. There, in a shallow depression beside a boulder or at the base of a tree, she lays eight to eighteen large eggs. The eggs are tan and speckled brown to blend with the leaves and stones on the ground.

Turkey egg shown actual size.

A month after they are laid,
the eggs hatch.

Baby turkeys are called poults. Very soon after they hatch, turkey poults are out of the nest and in the nearby grasses catching protein-rich insects they need for rapid growth.

The faster they grow the better off they are, in a world full of animals that like to eat turkeys. Turkey poults are killed by hungry foxes, coyotes, skunks, and owls.

As they grow bigger and stronger, young turkeys are less vulnerable to attack from small predators. A full grown turkey weighing fifteen to seventeen pounds is a powerful bird. It takes a coyote, wolf, bobcat, mountain lion, or human hunter to kill one.

Turkeys tend to run from danger, bursting into flight as a last resort.

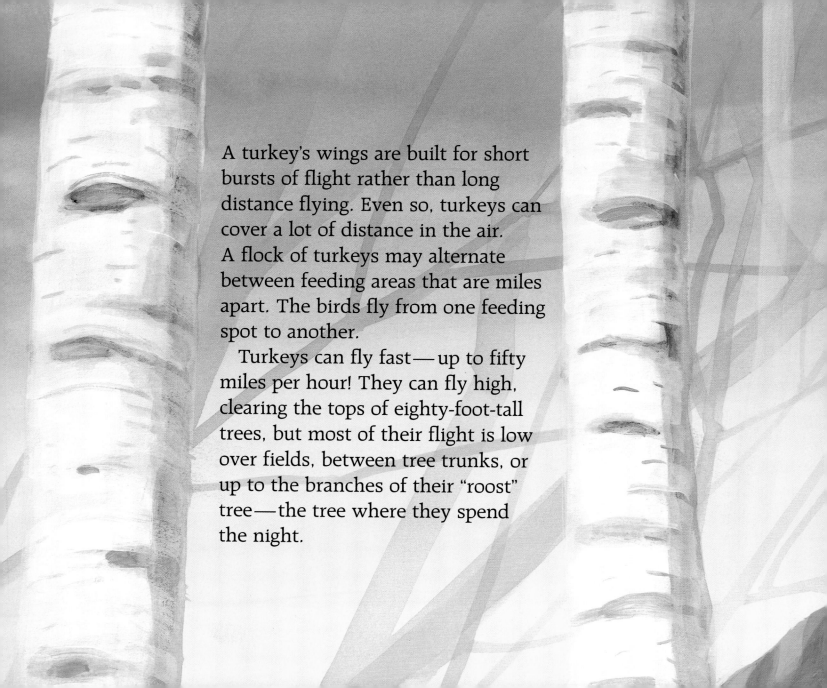

A turkey's wings are built for short bursts of flight rather than long distance flying. Even so, turkeys can cover a lot of distance in the air. A flock of turkeys may alternate between feeding areas that are miles apart. The birds fly from one feeding spot to another.

Turkeys can fly fast—up to fifty miles per hour! They can fly high, clearing the tops of eighty-foot-tall trees, but most of their flight is low over fields, between tree trunks, or up to the branches of their "roost" tree—the tree where they spend the night.

Turkeys are not winter migrators. They stay in the same general area all year long, sleeping in the same trees night after night, high and safe from most predators. Some roost trees are small, with limbs enough for only a half dozen turkeys. Other roost trees are large enough for a whole flock.

Turkeys are survivors. Even in places where deep winter snow covers the ground seven months of the year, resident flocks of turkeys make it through. Today the wild turkey can be found in the north, south, east, and west. After so many years of decline, the wild turkey is seen by more people, in more places, than ever before.

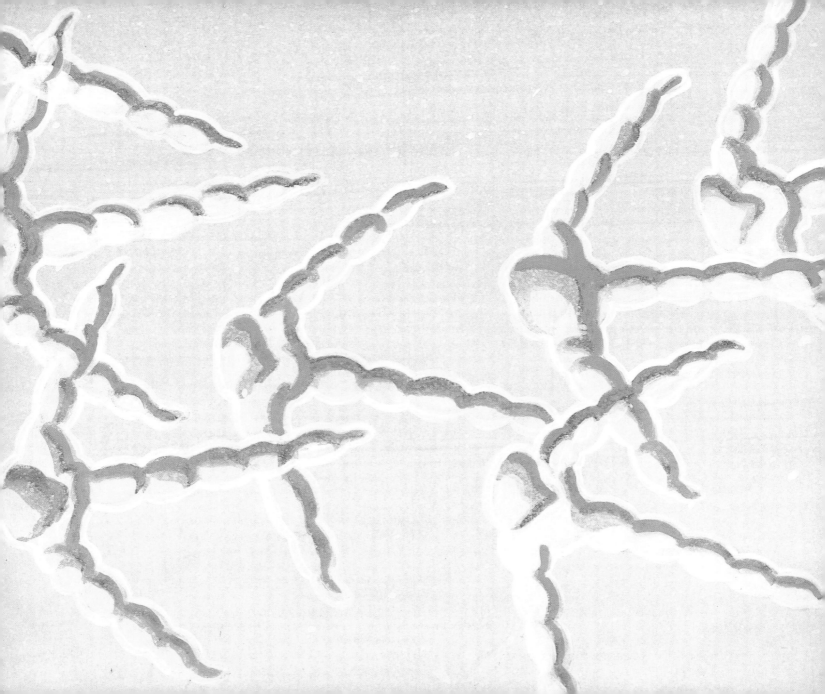